Pallet Furniture Plans You Can [Make at] Home

By

Carla Fowler

Pallet Furniture Design Plans You Can Build at Home

**Published by Designs by Pallet
Designs by Carla**

**ISBN-13:
978-1512285963**

**ISBN-10:
151228596X**

Carla Fowler

Table of Contents

1. **Pallet Furniture is For You** — 3
2. **Coffee Tables** — 5
3. **Pallet Iron Console Table** — 8
4. **Kitchen Island** — 10
5. **Pallet Rustic Bench** — 13
6. **Pallet Sofa on Wheels** — 16
7. **Pallet Porch Swing** — 19
8. **Pallet Kitchen Kart** — 22
9. **Pallet Kitchen Organizer** — 26
10. **Pallet Kitchen Spice Rack** — 29
11. **Kitchen Hanging Rack** — 32
12. **Pallet Kitchen Plate Rack** — 34
13. **Pallet Outdoor Kitchen** — 37
14. Conclusion — 39

Pallet Furniture Design Plans You Can Build at Home

Chapter One

Pallet Furniture is For You

I decided to write this book so people can see how easy it is to design and build their own Pallet furniture. Each chapter will highlight a different form of furniture that can be built out of pallets.

When you decide to build pallet furniture you must now go and get some pallets. There are places that will sell them to you. But there are many stores that simply throw them out behind their buildings. Just drive around your town and I assure you that you will find pallets that will make great furniture.

Carla Fowler

Before you go out and get pallets you must decide what shape pallets you need to make building easier. Pallets come in all shapes and sizes. When you collect all the pallets you need then assemble the tools you will need. A crowbar, hammer, screw drivers, nails, screws and any other items you feel you need.

Find an area of your home where you plan to build your furniture and turn into your studio. This way you can stop work and leave everything in place to make it easier to get started later.

For the rest of the book each chapter will describe a type of furniture and give some examples of different ways to build it. Use your Imagination the furniture you build is your creation so go wild and make it your creation.

Chapter 2
Coffee Tables

What are the main uses of a living room? Focused it is a versatile sitting area for your house, where you spend time, have coffee, watch movie, attend your guest. The most important part of the living room is the coffee table. A beautiful coffee table can change the entire look of the room. But it can not necessarily be expensive. Now the pallet coffee table is made for you not only in your budget, but also beautiful and unique.

Pallet coffee table is of two types. Firstly it is with the pallet wood top i.e. the coffee table's base and the top both are made up of the pallet wood. The second one is the pallet coffee table with a glass on top. This is very beautiful, as it gives a complete modern look to your living room. The base of the coffee table is made up of the pallet frame, and then that base is painted in the color which combines the whole interior of the room. The base can be decorated with flower vase or anything else you would like.

Pallet Furniture Design Plans You Can Build at Home

Carla Fowler

Chapter 3
Pallet Iron Console Table

If you are obsessed of wooden creativity then this given art style pallet table will make you more! Pallet wood has creatively been treated with raw iron scrap of home to produce this mind blowing DIY pallet and raw iron console for your family room, living room or media room. Iron metal scrap and lengths have been resized and welded to make a nice frame of this DIY pallet media console table having two levels.

Deconstructed pallet boards have been reclaimed to build the shelving levels of this raw iron frame of media stand. Accent headed screws have been added to hold the pallet planks in place to build a lasting design of pallet entertainment center on a budget! This grand media table can live with you for so many future years to avoid fading and wreathing it has been waxed and finished with varathane!

Chapter 4
Pallet Kitchen Island

Kitchen is the room of home that remains always in busy! It is the room for food preparation and should always be well organized to keep the kitchen paraphernalia and tools in touch! What can make a kitchen functional? This is really not difficult to tell, some special shelving and rack units and a functional kitchen island table are enough to make a kitchen functional and uncluttered. This handy design of DIY rustic kitchen island table is really beautiful and functional and has a zero cost price!

Some rustic and natural worn pallets have been ripped up, modified and refinished to gain this elegant style of distressed DIY pallet kitchen

Pallet Furniture Design Plans You Can Build at Home

table to assist you in quick preparation of food. Table design is so simple to achieve and contain two levels for a function demonstration. Make it painted using a bold paint shade or water base chalk to create its custom look for your shabby chic or modern chic interiors!

Carla Fowler

Chapter 5
Pallet Rustic Bench

Benches are always held pleasurable in home or at outdoor as we just feel relaxed by sitting back on them. My husband and I love to sit outside on the benches we make. Some home locations and areas always need a bench and home front porch is one of that places. If you are not able to by that manufactured versions and styles of benches then now you have an opportunity to gain a serviceable and study design of table at no-cost budget plan. This DIY pallet farmhouse bench has been constructed by reclaiming the old and weathered pallets.

Not only a lasting DIY pallet furniture element has been made but also the pallets skids have again brought to useful condition. So you should also use the pallets in home crafting as they have much feasible nature and can modified handily to get any utilitarian component of home furniture like a table, chair, stool, sofa or a bed frame. This DIY pallet front porch bench has been finished with water base poly to ensure its lifetime stability without getting fad or weather!

Pallet Furniture Design Plans You Can Build at Home

Chapter 6
Pallet Sofa on Wheels

How to change the deleted and retired pallets into great looking and pleasing furniture objects? This is really our great topic to discuss and we just feel passionate about it. As the world is growing more and more, the creative world of pallet wood is also making great progress. There are super examples of handcrafted furniture from pallets and people across the world are going to be more and more creative to reclaim the pallet wood for daily furniture essentials out of it just like this DIY pallet sofa with wheels, made with love and care and is just perfect for mature and toddler age group!

Pallet Furniture Design Plans You Can Build at Home

One complete pallet board gives the comfy berth sections of the sofa and armrests have been build using the thicker side bars of pallet boards, truly amazing piece of furniture to get your hands onto! This easy to move seat can serve you at multiple locations of home or even at patio. Wood has only been sanded for a bright charming look and has been finished with hardware wheels for a beautiful metal touch!

Carla Fowler

Chapter 7
Pallet Porch Swing

It is always super easy to plan the pallets for sitting furniture out of them. We have given here some highly knock out styles of pallet sitting furniture like chairs, loungers, pool side chairs, benches and also the swings. This time we are again with a fetching style of wooden swing, check this nice DIY pallet porch swing, supported with nautical rope that has further been fixed aloft with roof shaft. Simply make a DIY pallet sofa without legs and enable it for hanging by drilling the holes and fixing the hanging hardware and hooks through them.

Carla Fowler

Put up a heavy duty mattress or cushion and enjoy a dreamy life by lying or sitting on this super comfortable porch swing. This DIY pallet project of swing has been finished by making the design distressed with grey paint.

Pallet Furniture Design Plans You Can Build at Home

Chapter 8
Pallet Kitchen Kart

Take a little visit of the nearby landfills, junky yards and dumping grounds to get pallets. We assure you that by taking a look on our given list of DIY pallet furniture ideas you will surely find your vision come to life. Pallet wood is not less than a blessing to get functional furniture which is just impossible to buy in this age of inflation. You can build furniture for the visitors, guest and even for your sweet family. This project has drop leaves which can be added to get a classy counter space.

Pallet Furniture Design Plans You Can Build at Home

This amazing type of DIY pallet kitchen table has a storage cabinet, drawers and also the drop leaves to behave like a counter. This will really be adorable addition to your kitchen and will support you while transporting the kitchen food or other paraphernalia. A lot of care has been taking while designing the drop leaves of this amazing DIY pallet idea for a kitchen cart. These drop leaves are the most captivating part of the structure and give a magical look and a fashionable style to this kitchen cart.

Carla Fowler

Pallet Furniture Design Plans You Can Build at Home

Carla Fowler

Chapter 9
Pallet Kitchen Organizer

We have some rustic chunks of barn wood stored in our home scrape and we reclaimed them for a nice kitchen act. We prepared a DIY pallet kitchen organizer for kitchen tools and vegetable. This little pallet wood caddy can give some extra storage space to any room especially in kitchen. There are many options to gain its services in multiple ways. You can also make it hanged with some keyhole hangers at the back to kitchen wall to get a perfect DIY pallet rack for kitchen ware out of it. This is a use of pallets to build a organizer looks great as well.

Pallet Furniture Design Plans You Can Build at Home

This can be shown to any paint shade or color you want and will be highly serviceable kitchen. So get some old remains of pallet wood and go for crafting phenomenon of this pallet kitchen storage utility and enjoy it on a free of cost budget. We have coated it tow times to get this plane turquoise shade of color that makes it more precious and visually pleasing.

Carla Fowler

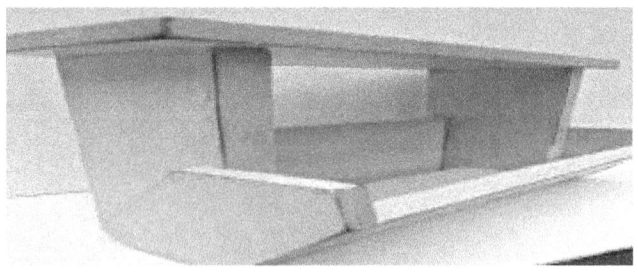

Chapter 10
Pallet Kitchen Spice Rack

Pallet wood can also be involved in reforming your kitchen by adding some DIY pallet kitchen shelves and some other functional wooden settings. This DIY pallet spice rack is also a great improvement for your kitchen and can hold on many of spices jars which are every time need of a kitchen. If you really want to remodel your kitchen in thrifty way then these DIY pallet shelves will be a great help and favor to you which is much less in budget.

We have nicely framed up pallet to behave as secured shelves and we have added a wooden dowel resistance and boundary to avoid falling of jars. You can simply get your hand on this functional DIY pallet product by using the lower

Carla Fowler

panel of the pallets and with a sanding. The fitting of wooden dowel stick can ask for some drill to make holes otherwise whole idea is much obtainable and thrifty.

Pallet Furniture Design Plans You Can Build at Home

Chapter 11
Pallet Kitchen Hanging Rack

Design some newly adopted designs for complete way setting of kitchen accessories. Our target would be a stands or shelves that can give true trendy fashion and best possible storage to kitchenware. Pallet wood can design for you such an arrangement for kitchen like pallet ganging rack. The hanging chain support of pallet rack gives trendy and reduced setting to the rack. You can hang your cooking tools on it starting with lovely one and which your need much time. The upper fine cut to the rack makes it more cute and charming. All supporting needs have been accomplished with hooks attachments.

Pallet Furniture Design Plans You Can Build at Home

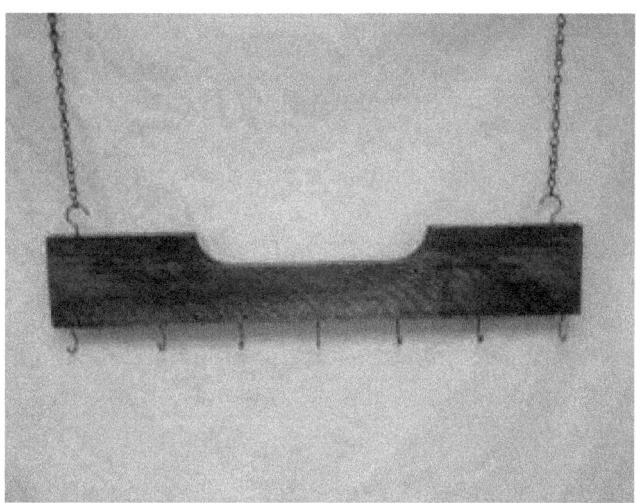

Chapter 12
Pallet Kitchen Plate Rack

Look for a wall panel in your home for a ceramic or clay plate set up. If you have left behind plates from sets that have broken, collect them and make a pleasing pallet plate rack display. Make a display rack from a shipping pallet and screw it in your dining room or morning room. Put in the colorful mixed and matched plates and secure them with rounded nails or wood chunks. Mix and match the size also or just go with one single color and add a pop of contrasting one. You can paint the pallet wood a matching color or leave it like that for a wood-ceramic look.

Pallet Furniture Design Plans You Can Build at Home

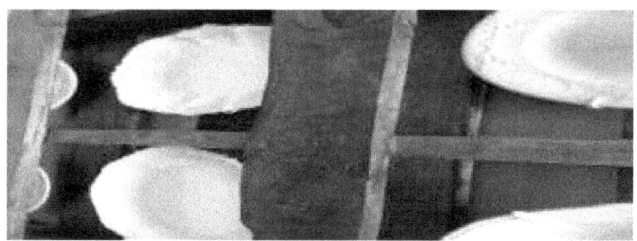

Carla Fowler

Chapter 13
Pallet Outdoor Kitchen

All of you certainly have seen many things made by recycled materials specifically the recycled pallets. I am sharing my work of pallet outdoor kitchen with all of you. There are many ways to design an outdoor kitchen look at some of these pictures and then let your imagination run wild.

Carla Fowler

Chapter 14

Conclusion

No matter what you decide to build enjoy the process. Building your own furniture will be a process you will not forget and the products you build will be some of your most loved. I hope some of my ideas will spark an idea that will create the piece of furniture you need.

CPSIA information can be obtained
at www.ICGtesting.com
Printed in the USA
LVHW050902050121
675674LV00020B/3395